Reading & Writing

Reading and Writing Today

Reading & Writing

Reading
and
Writing
Today

Marshall Cavendish
Benchmark
New York

This edition first published in 2009 in North America by Marshall Cavendish Benchmark.

Marshall Cavendish Benchmark
99 White Plains Road
Tarrytown, NY 10591
www.marshallcavendish.us

Library of Congress Cataloging-in-Publication Data

Silva, Patricia, 1963–
  Reading and writing today / by Patricia Silva.
     p. cm. — (Reading and writing)
  ISBN 978-0-7614-4324-7
  1. Written communication—Juvenile literature. 2. Writing—Juvenile literature. I. Title.
  P211.S617 2009
  302.2'244–dc22
                              2008032283

Text: Patricia Silva
Editing: Cristiana Leoni
Translation: Erika Pauli
Design and layout: Luigi Ieracitano
Illustrations: Alessandro Baldanzi, Alessandro Bartolozzi, Leonello Calvetti, Roberto Simoni
Maps: Roberto Simoni

Photographs: Scala Archives p. 14

Printed in Malaysia
1 3 5 6 4 2

Contents

Without Paper

Writing has undergone many changes over the centuries. From cuneiform clay tablets to richly illuminated medieval manuscripts to modern printed newspapers, the techniques of writing have evolved according to our needs and technological know-how.

Today, a great deal of writing is done through electronic media such as computers, PDAs (handheld computers), and cell phones. These new technologies allow a writer to compose a text, which is recorded onto a disk or chip. The reader, in turn, is able to access and read the text on a screen or monitor.

Who knows what new forms of writing man will invent in the future. One thing is certain: reading and writing will continue to evolve and change as we do.

Below: The home computer has made possible for people ⸱ read, write, and com municate across gre⸱ distances.

Opposite, top: Electronic books are available on the Internet. Readers can download entir⸱ e-books onto their computers and reac them on their monitors.

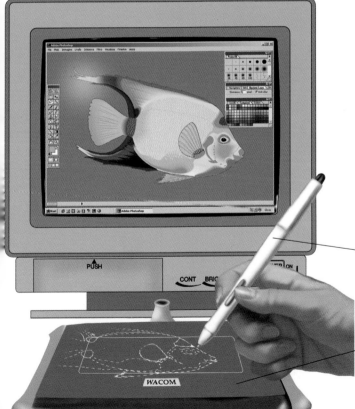

Left: Input devices, such as the electronic pen, allow for greater freedom in creating documents. Using this pen, a person can draw an image, which appears on the computer screen, and then manipulate the image in a variety of ways.

pressure-sensitive electronic pen

electronic drawing pad

7

In Few Words

Above: The copywrite[r] working alongside th[e] designer, is responsib[le] for writing the memo[-] rable phrases that hel[p] sell a product.

Left: In an advertisin[g] agency a creative tea[m] works to develop an advertising strategy, o[r] campaign, to promot[e] and sell their clients' products.

8

Advertising is all around us. Commercials yell out their messages on our TV screens, our roads are lined with bright billboards, and newspapers are filled with ads selling everything from cars to toothpaste.

Advertisements have been around since ancient times. Archaeologists working in Pompeii have even discovered campaign ads for political elections that took place almost 2,000 years ago. Today, advertising has become a multibillion dollar industry in which a television commercial broadcast during some sporting championships can cost as much as $75,000 per second!

Advertisers often use special forms of communication to sell their products. Have you ever found yourself humming the tune to an advertisement that you have seen on TV? These songs, or jingles, are written to help us recall the product being sold. Catchy phrases, called slogans, are also written in such a way to attract our attention and make us want to buy the product.

The Writing on the Wall

Have you ever wondered what that crazy writing you see on the walls of some buildings or on the side of some subway trains means? This writing is known as graffiti and it is a way some people use to express themselves publically to a large audience. Graffiti is used to protest, voice opinions, and express ideas.

The simplest form of graffiti is called tagging and is basically the signature of an individual graffiti artist. These signatures, or tags, are usually made-up names that the writers use to identify themselves. More complex forms of graffiti include protest slogans, thought-provoking sayings, and combinations of words with stylized images.

Above: Though it is always best to ask permission first, graffiti artist have traditionally used public spaces, such as walls, as canvases their messages.

Left: Some graffiti is created to honor special people—such as this example depicting the singer John Lennon— or causes that the writer feels are important.

Written in Lights

A modern "writing" material often used in advertisements is the neon sign. The idea for neon lights was first hinted at in 1675, when French astronomer Jean Picard noticed a faint glow coming from a tube filled with mercury gas. When Picard shook the tube it caused static electricity to light up the gas inside the tube. In the beginning of the 20th century, another Frenchman, Georges Claude, became the first to apply an electrical charge to a sealed tube of neon gas to create a neon lamp.

Modern neon signs are made by applying electrical charges to hollow glass tubes filled with different inert gases. Different colors are created by using different gases.

The most common color, red, is produced with neon gas. Blue is made with a mixture of argon and mercury gases; gold with helium; and white with carbon dioxide. Neon artists can also coat the inside walls of the glass tube with colored powders to produce additional color variations. Lastly, the tube itself can be made from colored glass, thereby producing very rich, saturated colored lights.

Left and opposite: Neon artists heat t glass tubes to very high temperatures until the glass becomes soft and malleable; then th

...t can shape the
...s into words,
...ges, and patterns.

Talking Balloons

At the end of the 19th century, a new type of literature became popular in America. The comic strip introduced readers to a whole world of imaginary characters and heroes. At first these characters appeared in comic strips in the Sunday supplements of newspapers, but as their popularity increased publishers . . .

Left: This drawing of Felix the Cat, a cartoon character first made famous in the 1920s, was done by pop artist Andy Warhol.

. . . began to produce entire comic books filled with the adventures and misadventures of such characters as Superman, Batman, Spiderman, and many others.

The comic strip is sequential. The narrative or story takes place in a series of drawings, usually within separate boxes . . .

Above: By giving human qualities to inanimate objects, or anthropomorphizing, the cartoonist is often able to make humorous observations regarding human behavior.

. . . called panels. The dialogue is written in compartments, called balloons, above the character's head.

Sound effects are included by using decoratively lettered onomatopoeia, or written words that imitate the sound they describe, such as SPLAATTT or BANG!

POW

The PC

The personal computer, or PC, has revolutionized how we write and communicate. The first computers, built in the 1940s, were extremely large—one filled an entire room! In the 1970s, MIT introduced a smaller, personal-sized computer called the Altair 8800, which was the "grandfather" of an entire generation of personal computers.

At first the PC was used mainly in offices to write documents, store and

Below: There are many components a personal comput[e]

picture tube

radiation shield

monitor

input/output portals

adjustable support

input (CD)

video connection

PC case

ke[y]

mouse

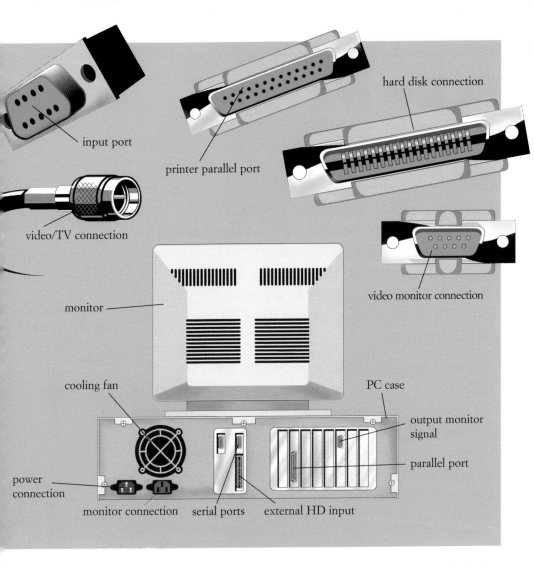

input port

printer parallel port

hard disk connection

video/TV connection

video monitor connection

monitor

cooling fan

PC case

output monitor signal

parallel port

power connection

monitor connection   serial ports   external HD input

rieve information, and complete complicated culations quickly, but as computers became more ordable and easier to use, home computers grew in pularity. The benefits of the PC soon increased. In following decades, computer technology made azing advances, allowing users to communicate oss great distances, view interactive imagery, com- se music, and much more.

Above: The back of a PC includes ports that allow the owner to connect external devices, such as monitors, modems, and printers.

By Way of a Screen

Almost every printed material that we read has passed through a computer screen. At one time, everything that was printed was first handwritten by a writer, then sent to a compositor, who manually arranged it by setting the text one letter at a time. Finally, the set text was sent to a printer for printing. Today all of these jobs can be done by one person using a computer.

This book that you hold in your hands, for example, was produced almost entirely using a computer. The text was written using a word-processing program and was then placed into a design program. A design program allows the designer to create the layout of a book by arranging text and images on the individual pages of his or her electronic document.

Once the designer has finished the layout, he or she can either print it out using a computer printer or can send the completed computer document, via CD or e-mail, to a printer for printing.

With a computer, text can be manipulated in an infinite number of ways. Its size, font, style, and color can be changed. Text can be stretched, condensed, or distorted according to the designer's ideas.

Preexisting images, such as photographs, illustrations, or maps, can be scanned and placed into the layout. New images can be drawn directly on the computer.

19

All Kinds of Disks

Just as books store written information, computers need a place to store their information. The hard disk drive, the CD, and the flash drive have all been developed for this purpose. The hard disk drive is located inside a computer and is used for the permanent storage of programs and data. People can both read and write information onto their hard disks.

CDs are thin disks of aluminum sandwiched between two protective layers of plastic. A CD can store fairly large quantities of information—approximately the equivalent of two complete sets of encyclopedias! The flash drive is a small, durable storage device that holds even more information than a CD and is much faster.

Below: A CD's aluminum layer is stamped with hollo areas and flat areas that together form code for the in mation bei written

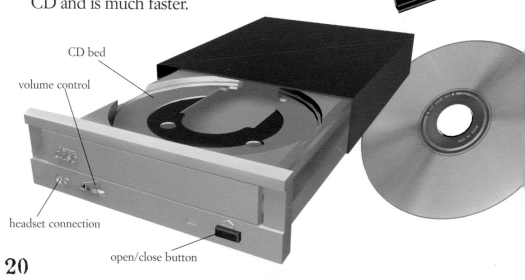

CD bed

volume control

headset connection

open/close button

power source
connection

IDE connection
to motherboard

·d
or
0
)

netized
or

ing

gold
plated
contacts

hard drive

Writing and Drawing

If you look around, you will see signs everywhere. Directional signs that help us find our way, promotional signs that indicate a particular store, and informational signs that help us find the restroom. Up until several years ago, most of these signs would have been hand-lettered.

Today, however, artists and designers are able to use several different computer programs to create their

PLACE
PHOTO
HERE

...twork. Programs such as Quark Xpress, ...ldus Freehand, InDesign, and Adobe ...hotoshop allow artists to create very ...ccurate texts and to manipulate images ... thousands of different ways.

...sing the program Photoshop, designers ...n scan a photograph onto their comput-
...s and then change the image to suit their ...eds. An image of a blue fish in a fishtank ...n be changed to show a yellow fish in ...e middle of an ocean. Images can be cut, ...asted, outlined, recolored, and distorted, ...hile texts can be colored, enlarged, reduced, and changed as needed.

Opposite: With a computer, drawings can be made using a variety of mark-making techniques. Your drawing can look like it was drawn with a pencil or painted with a brush.

23

E-mail

One of the earliest uses of the Internet was e-mail, which is short for electronic mail. As the name suggests, e-mail is a type of electronic letter that you can send and receive with your computer. To send an e-mail to a friend, you must first have his e-mail address, for example: john.smith@myfriend.com. The first part of this address is the user name that your friend has chosen to identify himself (john.smith). The second half is the domain name (myfriend.com), which tells your computer where your e-mail must be sent in order to reach your friend.

Once you have typed your message onto a computer, you click the "send" command on your e-mail program and your computer translates your message into a code that can be sent over the Internet to your friend's computer. Once there, your friend's computer reassembles the message so he or she can read it.

sende
server

modem

sender's
computer

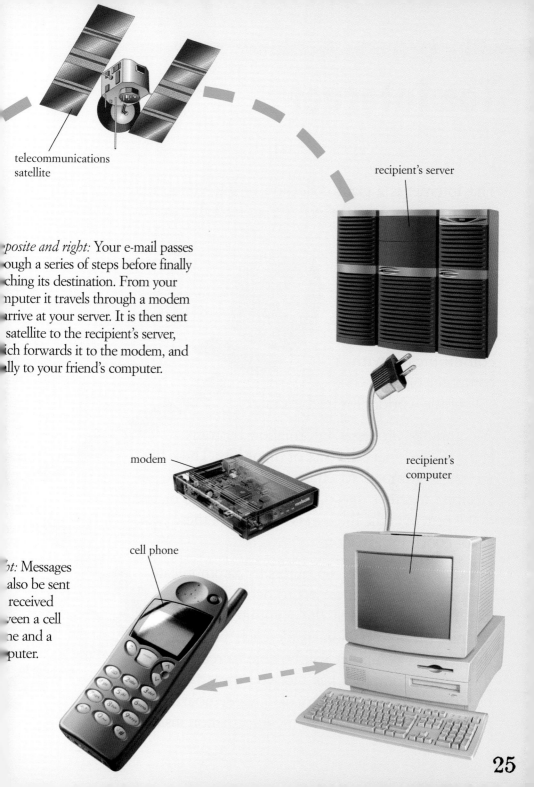

telecommunications
satellite

recipient's server

...posite and right: Your e-mail passes
...ough a series of steps before finally
...ching its destination. From your
...nputer it travels through a modem
...rrive at your server. It is then sent
... satellite to the recipient's server,
...ich forwards it to the modem, and
...lly to your friend's computer.

modem

recipient's
computer

cell phone

...t: Messages
... also be sent
... received
...veen a cell
...ne and a
...puter.

The Internet

The Internet is a giant collection of interconnected computer networks spread out around the world. These networks are connected using telephone lines, radio towers, and satellites. With the Internet, you can use your computer to communicate with a computer on the other side of the world. How is this done?

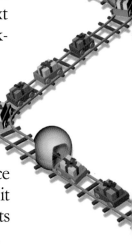

The message is sent from sender's computer

The message is divided into packets

A computer processes information by translating it into binary digits (1 or 0), or bits. These bits are then grouped together into bytes, which are grouped together into packets. Every image or text that is sent over the Internet is made up of these packets of coded information.

In order for different computers to communicate they use what are known as protocols. Protocols are like rules that tell the computer how to arrange the information inside each packet so that another computer will be able to read it. Once the second computer has received these packets, it uses the same rules of protocol to reassemble the bits and bytes to be able to read the information inside.

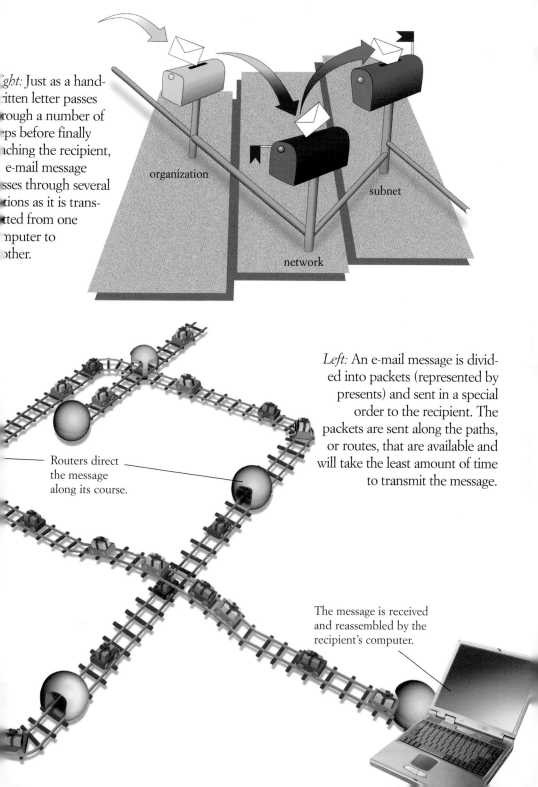

ght: Just as a handwritten letter passes through a number of steps before finally reaching the recipient, an e-mail message passes through several stations as it is transmitted from one computer to other.

organization

subnet

network

Left: An e-mail message is divided into packets (represented by presents) and sent in a special order to the recipient. The packets are sent along the paths, or routes, that are available and will take the least amount of time to transmit the message.

Routers direct the message along its course.

The message is received and reassembled by the recipient's computer.

Surfing the Web

The term *World Wide Web* (www) refers to a collection of files located on many different computers spread throughout the world. These files can contain a variety of information such as text, images, sound, and even computer programs. By using the Internet, people can view Web pages on their computers by simply accessing a browser (like Internet Explorer, Safari, or Firefox), which will translate the coded

Internet sites can be educational, like a museum or cultural site (*opposite*), or entertaining, like an interactive game website (*below*).

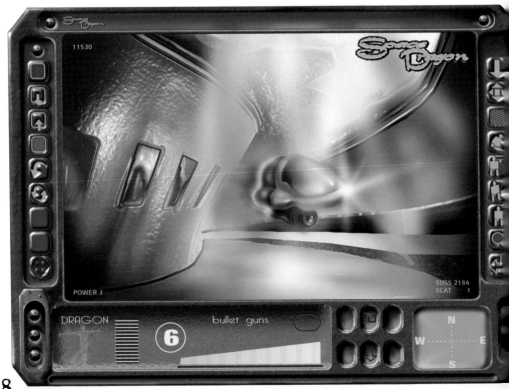

formation and display it on their omputer screens.

view a particular Web page, you ust have its URL, or Uniform esource Locator. The URL is a type address for the website and it tells ur computer where it can find the e you are looking for and how it n access that file. The URL for the uvre Museum in Paris looks like s: http://www.louvre.fr.

any Web pages contain links at allow the viewer to quickly nnect to other related Web ges. This movement from e link to another is referred as "surfing the Net." The rld Wide Web allows us access information, do earch, communicate h friends, and even y games.

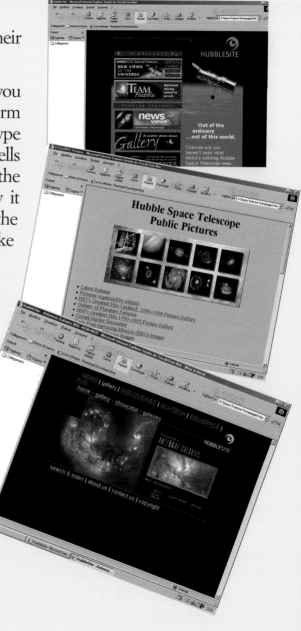

n a traditional book, each screen view website is called a page. The initial of a site is called the home page and lly has a directory, like a table of con-, of what can be found on that site.

Index

Page numbers in **boldface** are illustrations, tables, and charts.